TAYLOR LAUTNER

Maggie Murphy

PowerKiDS press.

New York

For my sister MG, who went to see Twilight *with me*

Published in 2011 by The Rosen Publishing Group, Inc.
29 East 21st Street, New York, NY 10010

First Edition

Editor: Jennifer Way
Book Design: Kate Laczynski

Photo Credits: Cover Jeff Kravitz/Film Magic/Getty Images; pp. 4, 5 Jason Merritt/Getty Images; pp. 6, 10, 27 Shutterstock.com; pp. 7, 11, 15, 17 Vince Bucci/Getty Images; p. 8 Frederick M. Brown/Getty Images; p. 12 Barry King/Wirelmage/Getty Images; p. 13 Frank Micelotta/Getty Images; p. 14 © Dimension Films/courtesy Everett Collection; pp. 16, 19, 22, 23, 24, 25 (bottom), 30 Kevin Winter/Getty Images; p. 18 © Maverick Films/Zuma Press; p. 21 © Imprint Entertainment/Zuma Press; p. 25 (top) Frazer Harrison/ Getty Images; p. 26 Michael Buckner/Getty Images for PCA; p. 28 Ezra Shaw/Getty Images; p. 29 Brendon Thorne/Getty Images.

Library of Congress Cataloging-in-Publication Data

Murphy, Maggie.
  Taylor Lautner / by Maggie Murphy. — 1st ed.
      p. cm. — (Movie superstars)
  Includes index.
  ISBN 978-1-4488-2564-6 (library binding) — ISBN 978-1-4488-2717-6 (pbk.) —
  ISBN 978-1-4488-2718-3 (6-pack)
  1. Lautner, Taylor, 1992—Juvenile literature. 2. Actors—United States—Biography—
Juvenile literature. I. Title.
  PN2287.L2855M85 2011
  791.4302'8092—dc22
  [B]
                                          2010028535

Manufactured in the United States of America

CPSIA Compliance Information: Batch #WW11PK: For Further Information contact Rosen Publishing, New York, New York at 1-800-237-9932

Contents

TWILIGHT STAR AND ACTION HERO

Here is Lautner at the opening of *The Twilight Saga: Eclipse* at the Los Angeles Film Festival in June 2010.

Taylor Lautner is a young actor. He has appeared in several movies, including *The Adventures of Sharkboy and Lavagirl, Valentine's Day,* and *Cheaper by the Dozen 2*. However, he is best known for his **role** as Jacob Black in *The Twilight Saga* movies.

Lautner is one of the highest-paid teen actors in Hollywood. He has many fans and has won several awards for his acting.

Although Lautner is famous for starring in the *Twilight* movies, he is also a rising star in the world of action movies. He hopes his upcoming roles in action films will make him into an action hero.

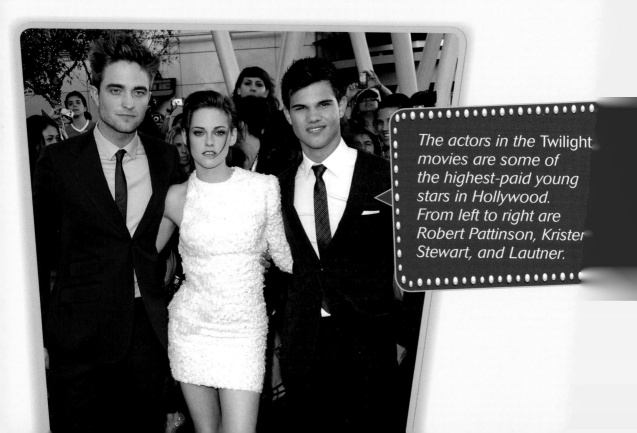

The actors in the Twilight movies are some of the highest-paid young stars in Hollywood. From left to right are Robert Pattinson, Kristen Stewart, and Lautner.

TAYLOR LAUTNER'S CHILDHOOD

Grand Rapids, Michigan, shown here, is the second-largest city in Michigan. Hudsonville, Michigan, where Taylor grew up, is a much smaller town.

Taylor Daniel Lautner was born on February 11, 1992, in Grand Rapids, Michigan. When he was four, his family moved to Hudsonville, Michigan. When Taylor was growing up, his mother, Deborah, worked for a software company.

His father, Dan, was an airplane pilot. Lautner is of French, Dutch, and German **heritage**. He is also part Native American on his mother's side. Lautner has a younger sister, named Makena.

Lautner played many sports growing up, including wrestling, football, and basketball. When he was six, he began taking karate lessons in Holland, Michigan. His **martial-arts** skills helped him get acting roles later.

Here is Taylor at age 13. He was going to the opening of a movie called Sahara.

GETTING INTO ACTING

Lautner's martial-arts training helped him become strong and graceful. This training can help him land roles as an action-movie star as his career grows.

When Taylor Lautner was 11, his karate coach told him that he should think about acting. The karate coach then sent Taylor to an **audition** for a Burger King commercial. Although Taylor did not get the part, he had fun auditioning. Soon, Taylor signed up with a talent **agency** in Los Angeles,

California, where many TV shows and movies are made. Taylor and his family flew there from Michigan a few times a month for auditions.

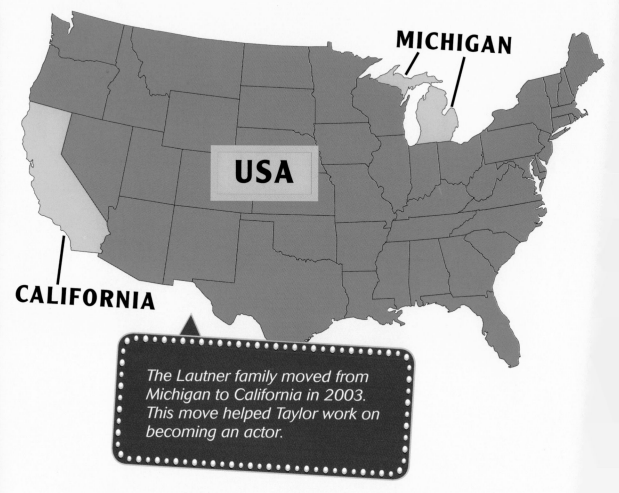

MICHIGAN

USA

CALIFORNIA

The Lautner family moved from Michigan to California in 2003. This move helped Taylor work on becoming an actor.

In the end, Taylor's parents asked him to choose between acting in Los Angeles or living in Michigan. Taylor did not want to give up acting, so the Lautners decided to move to Los Angeles

Hollywood is in Los Angeles. Many of the TV shows that Taylor was cast in were filmed in Hollywood.

in 2003. Soon, Taylor was cast in small roles on several TV shows. Between 2003 and 2004, Taylor appeared on episodes of *The Bernie Mac Show*, *My Wife and Kids*, *Summerland*, and *The Nick and Jessica Variety Hour*.

CARTOON VOICE WORK

After moving to Los Angeles and being cast in roles on TV shows, Taylor Lautner also started doing voice acting. Voice actors often provide the voices for animated characters on television and in movies. This is also called doing voice-over work. Voice actors generally

Here is Taylor at age 13, around the time that he did cartoon voice work for the show *Danny Phantom*

read from a **script** into a microphone. Then their voices are recorded and matched up with the action happening in the cartoons.

Taylor had success doing voice-over work for cartoon shows on television. Between 2005 and 2006, Taylor did voices for

Taylor is close to his family. Here he is with his sister, Makena, in 2005.

characters on *He's a Bully, Charlie Brown, The Adventures of Silas and Britney, What's New Scooby-Doo,* and *Duck Dodgers.*

However, one of Taylor's favorite voice-acting jobs was for a cartoon on Nickelodeon called *Danny Phantom* in 2005. For *Danny Phantom,* Taylor did the voice of Youngblood, a ghost pirate. Taylor has said he had fun making silly pirate noises for this role.

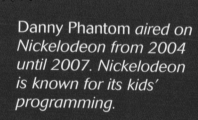

Danny Phantom *aired on Nickelodeon from 2004 until 2007. Nickelodeon is known for its kids' programming.*

Taylor's first leading role was in The Adventures of Sharkboy and Lavagirl. *His martial-arts training helped Taylor play Sharkboy, who saves the Planet Drool.*

When Taylor Lautner was 13, he was cast in his first major movie role, as Sharkboy in *The Adventures of Sharkboy and Lavagirl*. This movie is about a boy, Max, who dreams up two characters, Sharkboy and Lavagirl, who live in a world called Planet Drool. As Sharkboy, Taylor got to use his martial-arts skills to help save Planet Drool, in Max's imagination. The movie was directed by Robert Rodriguez. He also directed the *Spy Kids* movies. It opened in theaters in the summer of 2005.

Sharkboy and Lavagirl was very successful with movie **audiences**. In some theaters, the film was

Here is Taylor with (from left to right) actor George Lopez, director Robert Rodriguez, and actor Cayden Boyd at the Sharkboy and Lavagirl *movie opening in 2005.*

even shown with 3-D special effects. After the movie came out, Lautner says people started stopping him in the grocery store to ask if he was Sharkboy. His **performance** in the movie got the attention of directors and **producers** who wanted to cast him in more movies. It also got him many fans.

Sharkboy and Lavagirl *was Taylor's first big break. The attention he got from this movie helped him get cast in more movies.*

BREAKING OUT IN TWILIGHT

After playing Sharkboy, Taylor Lautner had a few more TV and movie roles. In 2006, Taylor played Eliot Murtaugh, one of the Baker family's neighbors, in *Cheaper by the Dozen 2*. In October 2008, Taylor appeared on TV with actor Christian Slater in *My Own Worst Enemy*.

Twilight was Taylor's next big break. Here he is signing autographs for fans at the opening of Twilight *in 2008.*

Lautner plays Bella Swan's friend Jacob Black in the Twilight movies. Here is Taylor as Jacob, with Gil Birmingham, who plays Jacob's father, Billy Black.

By the time *My Own Worst Enemy* appeared on TV, though, there was already a lot of talk about Taylor's role in a movie called *Twilight*. The movie was based on the first book in the popular book series of the same name. *Twilight* is about a teenage girl named Bella who falls in love with

Here is Taylor with some of his Twilight *castmates. From left to right they are Ashley Greene, Kellan Lutz, Nikki Reed, and Jackson Rathbone.*

a vampire named Edward. Taylor played Bella's friend Jacob Black, a Quileute Indian. *Twilight* opened in November 2008.

Playing Jacob in *Twilight* was Taylor's big break as an actor. The movie made more than $408 million in **box-office** sales worldwide. Taylor, along with the rest of *Twilight's* cast, quickly became very famous.

BECOMING JACOB BLACK

Taylor Lautner became famous for playing Jacob Black in *Twilight*. However, Jacob Black was almost played by another actor in the movie's **sequel**, *New Moon*. In *New Moon*, the character of Jacob becomes a **werewolf**. He is much taller and stronger than he was in *Twilight*. At first, the movie's director, Chris Weitz, did not think 16-year-old Taylor would be able to play Jacob in *New Moon* because he looked so young. Weitz considered using an older actor instead.

> Taylor had to become more muscular to play the werewolf Jacob Black in *New Moon*. *His hard work paid off, and Taylor won lots of new fans!*

SUPERSTAR FACT

In 2009, Taylor Lautner got to host *Saturday Night Live*.

Taylor started training to play Jacob in *New Moon* as soon as he finished filming *Twilight*. In order to keep his role as Jacob, Taylor had to become very **muscular**. He worked out between

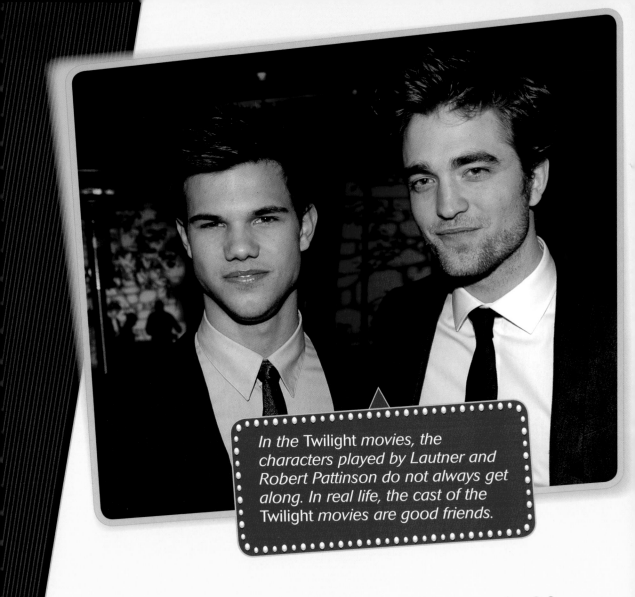

In the Twilight *movies, the characters played by Lautner and Robert Pattinson do not always get along. In real life, the cast of the* Twilight *movies are good friends.*

five and seven days a week in order to gain 30 pounds (14 kg) of muscle. In the end, Taylor was able to keep his role as Jacob. *New Moon* opened in theaters in November 2009.

MOVING BEYOND TWILIGHT

Taylor Lautner loves playing Jacob Black in the *Twilight* movies. However, he also wants to play different kinds of movie roles to show audiences and filmmakers that he is a **versatile** actor.

Lautner's first movie role after *New Moon* was in a 2010 romantic comedy called *Valentine's Day*. *Valentine's Day* starred many famous actors, such as Jamie Foxx, Julia Roberts, Jennifer

Garry Marshall directed Lautner in the 2010 movie Valentine's Day. *Lautner and Taylor Swift played high-school sweethearts in the movie.*

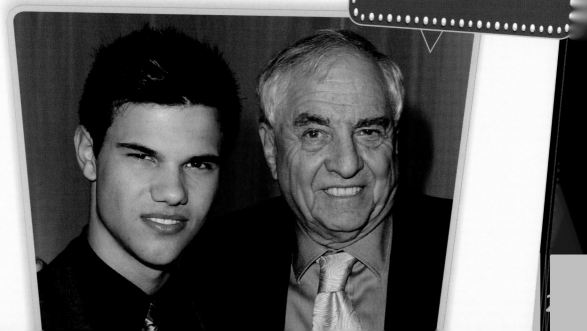

Valentine's Day *had a big cast. From left to right are Jennifer Garner, Emma Roberts, Shirley MacLaine, director Garry Marshall, Julia Roberts, Bradley Cooper, Ashton Kutcher, Carter Jenkins, and Jessica Biel.*

Garner, and Bradley Cooper. However, most of Lautner's scenes were with country-music star Taylor Swift. Although Lautner did not play a large role in *Valentine's Day*, he showed movie audiences that he could move beyond the character of Jacob Black.

ACTING AWARDS

Taylor Lautner has been **nominated** for many acting awards. In 2009, he was nominated for an MTV Movie Award for his performance in *Twilight*. He also won a Teen Choice Award that same year. In 2010, Lautner was nominated for two MTV Movie Awards for his roles in *New Moon* and *Valentine's Day*. He also won a 2010 Kid's

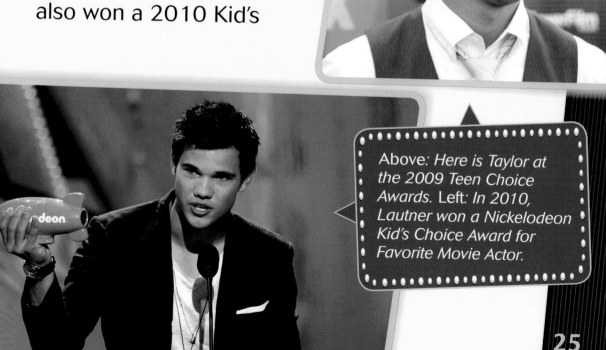

Above: *Here is Taylor at the 2009 Teen Choice Awards.* Left: *In 2010, Lautner won a Nickelodeon Kid's Choice Award for Favorite Movie Actor.*

Lautner also won a People's Choice Award in 2010.

Choice Award, as well as two 2010 People's Choice Awards.

Winning awards often catches the attention of directors and producers who want to cast popular actors in their films. Lautner is busy making and producing movies and is one of today's most popular young stars.

MARTIAL-ARTS CHAMPION

Studying martial arts has been a lifelong hobby for Taylor Lautner. When he was seven, he met a karate coach named Mike Chat at a national **championship** in Kentucky. Chat became Taylor's karate coach. In time, Lautner earned his black belt. He became a junior world champion at age 12.

Lautner has competed in martial-arts events since he was very young. At these competitions people show their skills by facing off against each other, as these two men here are doing.

Lautner wants to use his martial-arts skills to become an action movie star. He has said he would love to play an action hero role much like Matt Damon's role in the Jason Bourne movies. He is also a fan of the 2008 action thriller *Taken*, starring Liam Neeson. Many of Lautner's upcoming roles are in action movies.

TAYLOR LAUTNER'S FUTURE

Taylor Lautner is a very popular young actor. In 2010, he starred in *The Twilight Saga: Eclipse*. Lautner also has many upcoming film projects in addition to the *Twilight Saga* movies. He has a production company called Tailor Made. Having a production company gives him a way to find and work on projects that are

After movies have been made of all the Twilight books, Lautner wants to keep making movies. His production company, Tailor Made, will help him work on projects that interest him.

meaningful to him. Lautner has proven that he has a bright future as a Hollywood actor. His many fans cannot wait to see what he will do next!

Glossary

agency (AY-jen-see) A company that helps actors find work.

audiences (AH-dee-ints-ez) Groups of people who watch or listen to something.

audition (ah-DIH-shun) A test of the abilities of a performer.

box-office (BOKS-o-fus) Having to do with the money a movie makes.

championship (CHAM-pee-un-ship) A contest held to decide the best, or the winner.

heritage (HER-uh-tij) Parents and other relatives.

martial-arts (mar-shul-ARTS) Several types of self-defense or fighting that are practiced as sport.

muscular (MUS-kyuh-lur) Strong.

nominated (NO-muh-nayt-ed) Suggested that someone or something should be given an award or a position.

performance (per-FAWR-ments) The playing of a role in a movie, play, or TV show.

producers (pruh-DOO-serz) People who make movies and TV shows.

role (ROHL) A part played by a person in a movie, play, or TV show.

script (SKRIPT) The written story of a play, movie, radio, or TV show.

sequel (SEE-kwel) The next in a series.

versatile (VER-suh-tul) Having the ability to do many things well.

werewolf (WIR-wulf) In myths, a person who can turn into a wolf or a wolflike creature.

★Index

★Web Sites